RANDALL'S RULES

The Definitive Guide For Successfully Navigating The Coaching Profession

VOLUME TWO

COACH MORGAN RANDALL

LEGAL NOTICE EVEN COACHES DARE NOT IGNORE!

Coach Morgan Randall

Randall's Rules volume one

Copyright © 2018 by Coach Morgan Randall

All rights reserved. No part of this book may be reproduced or transmitted in any for or by any means, electronic or mechanical, including photocopying, recording or by any information storage and retrieval system, without express written permission from the publisher, except for the inclusion of brief quotations in critical articles or a review.

Because this book is an entertainment product, it is not a substitute for professional advice on the topics discussed in it.

You are advised to do your own due diligence when it comes to making any decisions. Use caution and seek the advice of qualified professionals before acting upon the contents of this book. You shall not consider any examples, documents or other content in this book or otherwise provided by the author or publisher to be the equivalent of professional advice. The author and publisher assume no responsibility for any loses or damages resulting from your use of any information contained in this book.

Request for permission should be made in writing or online to:

    Coach Morgan Randall

    Radnor University

    www.CoachMorganRandall.com

    info@CoachMorganRandall.com

Library of Congress Control Number: 2018966898

ISBN: 978-0-9850671-7-5

Printed in the United States of America

PRAISE AND SHAMELESS SELF-PROMOTION FOR RANDALL'S RULES

"Coach Randall is the most famous person you've never heard of and his new book is great."
-John Doe

"Reading this book will provide you with a solid foundation."
-Bill Ding

"I think he was drunk when he wrote this."
-Bud Wiser

"I predict your future will be much brighter after you read this."
-Crystal Ball

"You'll become a much stronger leader after reading Randall's Rules."
-Dick Tater

"Reading this book helped me find a couple extra hours in my day."
-Earl Lee Riser

"This book will stop you in your tracks."
-Stan Still
"One of the funniest books I've ever read."
-Hugh Morris

"Worth every penny."
-Hy Price

"Coach Randall shows you an unorthodox path to get from where you are to where you want to be."
-Jay Walker

"I really appreciate all the rules about equipment."
-Jim Locker

"Randall's rules will help you level up
your program a little bit."
-Justin Miles North

"I enjoy listening to the audiobook when I'm commuting in my Explorer."
-Lewis N. Clark

"There are some people whom this book
simply can't help."
-Noah Vail

"Reading this will make you feel like Morgan has an uncanny ability to
predict your future."
-Horace Scope

"If your program or career has fallen on hard times, this is just the thing
to help."
-Neil Down

"If you're a coach, you can't
afford not to read this."
-Price Wright

"Affluent coaches might even
find this helpful."
-Rich Mann

"Read this today."
-Tom Morrow

"A great book to enjoy on a hot summer day."
-Virginia Beach

"If you don't like it, I'll give you your money back."
-Warren T.

DEDICATION

This book is dedicated to you. I want you to avoid the mistakes, bumps, bruises and embarrassments I've experienced over the years in my travels.

ACKNOWLEDGMENTS

Special thanks to everyone who didn't endorse this book.

INTRODUCTION

Thank you for investing in volume two of Randall's Rules. This resource is comprised of hard learned lessons that are a testament to the occupational hazard that comes with the territory of being a road warrior.

With that said, hopefully you already know some of the hazards come with the territory. This book will help you avoid the other ones. You're probably wondering how I might know about all of these. Quite simply, I've made every mistake in the book. At least twice. So, hopefully I will help you avoid many of the dangers and frustrations of life on the road as a coach and world-class recruiter.

*Disclaimer: These rules are not a substitute for advice or consultation with a physician, dietician, psychologist, psychiatrist or any other type of medical professional whose job title ends in "cian" or "ist".

RULE #93

TRAVEL WITH A BOTTLE OF FEBREZE FABRIC REFRESHER.

I recommend the extra strength original scent. It helps get rid of well, just about any odor you'll encounter in a hotel or dorm room. Pet smells, stale beer, body odor, smoke and it works on furniture, upholstery, carpets, rugs and any other item that's hard or downright impossible to wash. They make a 2.8 oz travel size hand held container and a larger 27 ounce spray bottle. Do yourself a favor get both.

(Division I coaches probably don't have to worry about this rule either since they stay in five star hotels while sipping champagne and eating caviar. And you wonder why the rest of us don't like you.)

RULE #94
DON'T LET AN ASSISTANT COACH COMPLETELY CHANGE THE IDENTITY OF YOUR PROGRAM.

It's his/her job to improve what your program already is, polish it up and make it shine a little brighter. I've seen head coaches give too much freedom, authority and responsibility to assistants. They've trusted their opinion a little too much and it's come back to bite them in the rear. Many assistant coaches are only in the business because they were college athletes, recently graduated and still don't know what they want to be when they grow up. Others are simply coaching while getting their graduate school paid for before they go off into the real world. Heck if you add up the cost of their tuition waiver, stipend, room and board they probably make more than you do. As a result, it's a good idea not to give them too much responsibility too soon, as no one will work harder for your program than you and at the end of the day it's your job on the line.

RULE #95

PRESS YOUR TONGUE AGAINST THE BACK OF YOUR TEETH TO PREVENT A SNEEZE.

(I'M A FOUNTAIN OF USELESS KNOWLEDGE. YOU'RE WELCOME.)

RULE #96
GO PEE BEFORE YOU GET ON THE ROAD.

Seriously, whether it's a trip on the team bus, 15 passenger van or just sharing a rental car. Go to the bathroom and empty your tank BEFORE getting in the vehicle. If you don't you will be the one person who makes everyone else late because you have to stop and take a leak. Then everyone will be pissed. (No pun intended. Okay maybe punned intended.)

RULE #97
EAT WHENEVER YOU CAN, ESPECIALLY IF IT'S FREE.

Whenever you're traveling per diem meal money doesn't go very far at all. And to add insult to injury food is one of your biggest expenses. At the small school level you don't get the luxury of being a fussy eater and your time on the road will beat that habit right out of you.

Instead of wasting time to stop and eat on the road, plan your travel around free meals. Most hotels offer a free continental breakfast. Hampton Inns are a personal favorite because they include a free hot breakfast as well as free coffee and cookies all day. Always grab a cup of joe and a couple cookies to go, you'll want them later. Schedule your departure time early (or late) enough to eat the free hotel breakfast. The rooms were already paid for so you may as well take advantage of the free meals. Depending on where you're traveling, the hotel meal might be the most balanced, healthy food option of your day compared to truck stops and rest area vending machines. So never and I repeat NEVER pass up a free meal.

Same holds true for postgame tailgate parties. Parents and boosters love cooking, baking and grilling for their student-athletes. These postgame events are a great opportunity for your team to get fed for free and also build relationships with the fans and boosters. There are plenty of other creative ways to reduce food costs on the road, you simply need to get creative. (That being said, your team will quickly begin to hate hotdogs and hamburgers because that's the most common, cheap and easiest way to feed an army full of 35-50 athletes.)

RULE #98

PUTTING DEODORANT ON A MOSQUITO BITE WILL STOP THE ITCHING.

RULE #99
NEVER CRY IN PUBLIC.

Not on field after an injury, not in the stadium after a loss, and certainly not during an emotional post-game interview with mics and cameras in your face.

It's crazy I even have to freaking mention this but I've seen each of these happen before and it wasn't pretty. Today more so than ever before, the camera is always on.

RULE #100
Q.W.D.
(QUICK WALKING DISTANCE)

Always stay within quick walking distance from the team bus, hotel, stadium, campus, or whatever venue you've traveled to especially after dark.

It's never a good idea to venture off and explore an unfamiliar city, especially at night and especially alone. The last thing you want to have happen is to walk from the hotel to a restaurant that the hotel front desk person recommended which ends up being on the other side of town and further away than you thought. Only to encounter a group of unsavory looking "townies" who either want to recruit you into their gang or rob you blind and leave you for dead in a dark alley.

This happened to me in Poughkeepsie back in the 80's. Fortunately a cop car drove by and I practically threw myself in front of it. I know you think "this would never happen to me" but what if you can't call an Uber and your cell phone battery is dead. You're now stranded somewhere you don't want to be. Your safest bet is to stay with the bus driver. It's not like the team can leave without him.

RULE #101

IF YOU DON'T HAVE A FLASH LIGHT ON YOUR PHONE TAKE A PICTURE OF THE SUN AND USE THE PHOTO TO FIND YOUR WAY IN THE DARK.

RULE #102
ALWAYS TAKE FANS AND BOOSTERS SERIOUSLY.

Anything you say can and will be held against you in the court of public opinion and on social media.

#I'mNotKidding

RULE #103
BUDGET STRETCHERS

When you need electronic equipment but don't have enough money in your budget, buy the item at the store, open it then promptly return the item. Check back at the store in a day or two to see if the item is on the "open box" or clearance table.
Then buy it again but this time it will be for 30% off.

A similar strategy works for online purchases. When you're buying something on sites like Craigslist.com, send a few insultingly low ball offers from burner email accounts then send a reasonable but not great offer from your real email address.
It will usually be accepted by the seller.

RULE #104
AN OUNCE OF PREVENTION IS WORTH A POUND OF CURE.

The divorce rate among major college coaches in football and basketball is between 75-50%. So, instead of getting married just find a woman you hate and give her your house.

RULE #105
THERE'S NO SUCH THING AS REJECTION

If you're feeling a little road weary and beaten down on the recruiting trails try shifting your perspective. A recruit choosing to sign with a different institution didn't reject you or your program. There's actually no such thing as rejection.

Some prospects will want what you have to offer, some will not. But understand that the ones who don't want it aren't rejecting you. They just want something else. This isn't rejection it's merely a good reminder for you that you should only be looking for those select few who are looking for precisely what you have to offer. Besides, the fact that they didn't sign with you may say more about them than it does about you.

If a recruit chooses to commit elsewhere, it's just the universe's way of protecting you from something or somebody that wasn't a great fit. It actually frees up room (and scholarship money) for someone who is. Don't chase, attract. Big difference. This eliminates fear of rejection and replaces it with a sense of empowerment and control.

*If you're single, please note that this rule also applies to dating.

(P.S. Tinder is not "dating".)

RULE #106
PLAY DUMB.

It worked for Ben Matlock, Columbo and Sargent Schultz. (Millennials won't get those television show references.)

This rule is so important I probably should've made it number one. It's vital to your sanity and survival. Don't know how to do anything that doesn't DIRECTLY pertain to your job as a coach. This is mission critical to your own self-preservation. Don't believe me? Go back into your files and find the employment contract you signed but probably didn't read too carefully.

The last clause in coaching contracts almost always reads something like this:

"Performs any other related duties as assigned by the Athletic Director or other appropriate administrator."

How confident am I that your contract says that? A Google search of that exact phrase yielded **41,100,000 results in 0.65 seconds.** And if it's not in the contract it sure is in your job description.

Athletic directors are masters at squeezing at least three nickels out of every dime. This is why you never want to drop a hint that you know how to update a website or use StatCrew software. You may find yourself becoming the assistant sports information director.

If you happen to mention that you know how to use Front Rush you very well might become the recruiting coordinator for the entire athletic department. And if someone discovers your video editing skills you'll find yourself being forced to become the athletic department videographer. Look like you know what you're doing in the weight room and you'll be the strength coach before you know it.

That's right, no good deed goes unpunished in higher education. Ten times out of ten adding job responsibilities doesn't come with a pay increase. You're better off playing dumb like Columbo or Matlock and just being just the 'football guy' or that 'basketball maven'.

RULE #107

EMPTY CEREAL BOXES MAKE GREAT MAGAZINE HOLDERS.

RULE #108

DON'T TRY TO BECOME FRIENDS WITH THE SPORTS INFORMATION DIRECTOR.

It will just make him hate you more. He already despises you because every time you play a game it creates a ton of work for him. Don't make it worse.

RULE #109

WHEN STUCK IN TRAFFIC, DON'T TRY AND OUTSMART THE GRIDLOCK.

Yeah, I know you're in a hurry to get to the game or don't want to be late for the home visit. But when you're stuck in traffic the best thing you can do is stay on the planned route. Yes, I also know you've got Google maps and the Waze app that crowd sources traffic jams and you can probably find an alternate route but doing that will come back to haunt you and here is why:

1. By taking an alternate route, you're alleviating the traffic for others not necessarily for yourself. What if you get off the highway and onto a road buses and trucks can't travel on?
2. Do you really think you're the only person with that idea? There will be tons of other vehicles trying to get off the highway to go around the congestion.
3. What if you get lost by opting to take a backroad or stuck in more traffic on a different road.
4. While all of this is going on whatever caused the traffic jam is either being fixed or removed from the roadway.
5. Just stay on the planned route and be patient. It beats getting lost or delayed on a different road trying to go around the gridlock.

RULE #110

DO IT YOURSELF BOTTLE OPENER.

To open your beer while driving *(I'm talking about passengers only here)* use the metal end of your seat belt buckle.

In a hotel and forgot your bottle opener for the 6-pack you bought? Using this same concept, open your room door and look at the door frame lock-plate, the hole for the latch works amazingly well as a bottle opener.

RULE #111
TAKE FOOD TO GO EVERY CHANCE YOU GET.

Whether you're hungry or not. If the team stops at Olive Garden and you're full, get an order of breadsticks to go, you'll be hungry later and want it. If there's a post-game tailgate when the party is over take all the leftovers with you because you and others team members will be hungry later and there either won't be a place to stop or time to stop on the way home.

RULE #112
IGNORE PLAYERS PARENTS.

Just because a dad won his fantasy league doesn't mean he can actually coach a real team. Just my observation.

RULE #113
DO IT YOURSELF WIRELESS HEADPHONES.

Wireless headphones are super popular but they're also super expensive. Get a pair of wire cutters and use them to quickly make any set of headphones wireless.

(I just saved you about $150. You're welcome.)

RULE #114

A BEAT UP, FADED, DENTED PICK-UP TRUCK IS COOL. BEAT UP, FADED, DENTED ATHLETIC EQUIPMENT ISN'T.

Take care of your gear. Look good, feel good, play good.
(Or if you're an English teacher... look good, feel good, play well.)

RULE #115
YOUR NETWORK IS YOUR NET WORTH.

Make friends with as many coaches as you can. To have a long, prosperous career your connections in the profession will be one of your greatest assets.

Respected coaches of established programs call on their closest colleagues in the coaching fraternity when they have a vacancy on staff. Your name won't be in the mix for these opportunities if you're not out there networking and building a solid reputation in the coaching profession.

A lot of people are very critical of the coaching profession because of its politics. Don't be one of those people. All you have to do is be outgoing, easy to get along with, helpful and highly professional on and off the field. It's fairly simply, no matter how much people try to complicate it.

RULE #116
DO IT YOURSELF BLUE TOOTH.

Tuck your iPhone under your headband or baseball cap to make your device hands free.

Note: Unfortunately this does not work on Android devices.

RULE #117
FIND FREE WIFI PASSWORDS ON FOURSQUARE.

FourSquare is a website and app where people share tips, ratings and reviews on places to go near you (places like restaurants, coffee shops, bars).

The most valuable part of this website is the "Tips" section where people can leave helpful recommendations for other travelers.

It's often here that you'll find the WiFi password for places. So, if you have don't have unlimited data because you're not a big time Division One coach and need WiFi in a pinch, you can easily jump on Foursquare and snoop around for WiFi passwords.

RULE #118
THERE'S ANOTHER APP FOR THAT.

WiFi Map is an app that shows you the passwords to different WiFi networks (over 100 million of them they say). The great part is that they've organized on a map so you can easily scope out the ones closest to you.

*Note: Some disgruntled users report that passwords are outdated, but it's still a handy tool to have in a pinch.

RULE #119

STOP YOUR DOG FROM PULLING ON THE LEASH BY SIMPLY WALKING FASTER.

RULE #120

EXTRA STRENGTH TRIPLE ACTION GOLD BOND POWDER IN THE GREEN CAN IS A GIFT FROM THE COACHING GODS.

Don't leave home without it. What is it? It's like baby powder on steroids. You may want to buy stock in this company. Especially in the summer during camp season.

Whether you're wearing flip flops or turf shoes, it's a fact of life that your feet will start to smell. Dumping some Gold Bond on them is a quick way to deodorize and make you feel human again.

It's also great to use in your drawers as it can keep swamp ass at bay for most of the day.

RULE #121
THE SOMETIMES-ALWAYS-NEVER RULE

- Athletic directors will sometimes allow you to go over budget.
- They always expect you to fundraise and do more with less resources.
- They never raise your operating budget.
- And gentlemen, this rule also applies to jacket buttons on suits and sports coats.
- The top button should sometimes be buttoned (depending on style).
- The middle button should always be buttoned.
- The last button should never be buttoned (it makes you look like an idiot and messes with how your jacket looks on you in terms of fit).

RULE #122

WHEN YOU'RE DOWNLOADING A FILE, FLIP YOUR SCREEN SIDEWAYS SO GRAVITY HELPS THE DOWNLOAD.

RULE #123

SAVE TIME AND NEVER LOSE YOUR KEYS EVER AGAIN.

Leave your house key in your front door lock and leave your car key in the ignition.

I conservatively estimate this has saved me at least the equivalent of three years' worth of time over the course of my life. (That's 26,280 hours.)

RULE #124
NEVER BUY TEXTBOOKS AGAIN.

This is a tip for your players and graduate assistants. Don't buy overpriced textbooks while you're in college, check them out of the college library instead. If they don't have them, order them on inter-library loan.

#Division3Problems

RULE #125
DON'T WASTE MONEY ON SKIMMED MILK.

Just buy whole milk and add a lot of water to it. This way you'll get so much more for the same price.

RULE #126

PROACTIVELY ENGAGE IN PROFILING BEFORE YOU GET IN THE AIRPORT SECURITY LINE.

Always get behind business travelers when in security lines. They move fast since they are usually in a rush and travel light. They know the drill. Line up behind them as much as possible. You'll speed through the line!

Never get behind families. They take forever. It's not their fault, they just have a lot of stuff because of the kids. Car seats, strollers, back packs, toys, and you'll notice it's always the dad carting every last piece of it like he's some sort of Sherpa or pack mule. (Dad's always get the short end of the stick.) At all costs try to avoid getting in lines with lots of families and kids. It's going to take a while.

RULE #127
RENT-A-CHAIR

While we're on the subject of airport security lines and baggage (emotional or otherwise) let's address something. So you're not that jerk slowing the line down to a crawl, when you're flying to recruiting camps and showcases, instead of bringing your camp chair and paying to send it through baggage claim, do this…

As soon as you land, buy a chair at the local Walmart (keep the receipt) use it for the weekend and return it right before you fly back home. Repeat each trip.

Note: If you're a Division One coach you can disregard this rule or if you're even more pretentious than most of your D-1 brethren just replace Walmart with Ethan Allen and camp chair with leather recliner and have at it.

RULE #128

FOCUS

Save money on expensive binoculars by just standing closer to the object you want to look at.

RULE #129
EAT AT EXPENSIVE RESTAURANTS DURING LUNCH.

Many expensive restaurants offer lunch specials featuring close to the same food they would serve for dinner but for half the price. Lunch time is seriously the best time to eat out when you travel.

RULE #130

ALWAYS HAVE AN EXTRA USB CHARGER OR EXTERNAL POWER PACK.

Batteries die, good moods shouldn't.

RULE #131

SAVE MONEY ON DOCTOR VISITS BY NOT GETTING SICK OR INJURED.

RULE #132
NO OUTLETS?

If you're at a hotel and run out of outlets to charge your phone, use the USB port on the back of the television.

RULE #133
WHAT'S IN YOUR WALLET?

Get a credit card with great reward points, buy all your team's athletic equipment and apparel on it and redeem the points and miles for free travel to take your family on vacation each year.

This might be the only way Division Three coaches can afford to take a vacation. Plus, everything's more fun when someone else is paying for it.

RULE #134

SAVE MONEY ON GAS BY WANTING TO BE WHERE YOU ALREADY ARE.

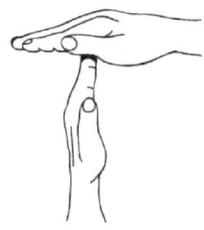

TIME OUT

We interrupt your regularly scheduled programming to bring you this important announcement about WD-40. Little do you know but WD-40 is about to become the most valuable player in your program. Read rules #135-160 and it will revolutionize the way you solve problems.

(You can thank me later.)

WD-40

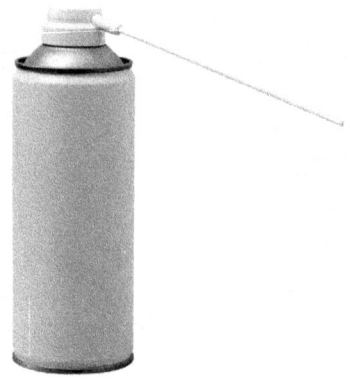

WD-40 was invented by three founders of the Rocket Chemical company in San Diego California. One of the founders Norman Larsen was attempting to create a solvent that would prevent corrosion of the outer parts to the Atlas missile in the aerospace industry.

He literally got the formula right on the 40th attempt and decided to name it Water Displacement 40th Attempt or WD-40.

RULE #135
DRY-ERASE BOARDS

The number one use you will find for WD-40 is removing permanent marker from dry erase boards. It's happened to all of us, an idiot freshman or Juco transfer goes to draw something up on the board and has no clue they can't use a sharpie on the dry erase board. You don't need to throw the board away, just spray a little WD-40 on the board and wipe it off. Then apply dry erase cleaning spray to the board so the WD-40 residue doesn't make the board too greasy to write on.

(You're welcome)

RULE #136
METAL GOALS

The second best use for it is for soccer, lacrosse and hockey coaches. If you coach one of these sports WD-40 is blessing for metal goals. It removes rust and oxidation from your goals

(and also metal furniture).

RULE #137
SEATING

It can also be used to protect plastic benches from sun damage or rain.
You've probably seen how the sun causes cracking and color fading on your outdoor seating at the athletic facility.

To protect it just spray a little WD-40 on the plastic and wipe it clean with a dry rag. Even if the seating is already a little worse for the wear from the sun and elements a little dab of WD-40 will recondition and give it a little more shine.

RULE #138
HELMETS

Share this one with your equipment manager. If you've ever removed a helmet decal you know how annoying it is to be left with that disgusting, sticky smudge mark that's left after the sticker is mostly gone. Just spray a little WD-40 on that area and use a clean rag to wipe it off. Voila!!! The mark is gone.

RULE #139
CELL PHONE SCREENS

Fixing cracked cell phone screens. Well, it won't completely repair the crack or scratches but it WILL improve the appearance of the screen. All you've got to do is spray it on and wipe it off with a clean dry cloth. If you're a small college coach, it will at least buy you some time until you can afford a new phone.

RULE #140
DAMN SQUIRRELS

I learned this trick from Mrs. Coach Randall. The damn squirrels in the yard drive her nuts. (see what I just did there) They steal the bird seed out of the bird feeders and make a mess everywhere in the process.

All you need to do to prevent this is spray a little squirt of WD-40 on the pole or hanger your bird feed sits on and the squirrels will slide right off when they try to climb it and steal food.

RULE #141
GENTLEMEN

Guys, don't tell your wife I told you this but WD-40 is great at removing lipstick from your shirt collars. Plus, if you're coming home too late, you can spray WD-40 on squeaky door hinges to silence them so no one hears you enter the house.

RULE #142
LADIES

Gals, don't tell your husband I told you this but WD-40 is great at removing a ring that's stuck on your finger. Yeah, I know you know liquid soap works but WD-40 is the quickest and easiest way to loosen up a ring and remove it from your finger.

All you've gotta do is spray a little around the ring and slide it right off. You probably will want to wash your hands thoroughly afterwards.

RULE #143
PARENTS & KIDS

For those of you with young children, WD-40 does a great job at removing scuff marks and crayon from walls. Spray some WD-40 onto a washcloth or paper towel and using a little elbow grease, wipe the marks. The crayon should buff out rather quickly.

It also works well to separate stuck lego blocks, just be sure to clean them before giving them back to the kid.

Old Coach Tip: Make them clean up their own damn mess or you'll be doing it for them until they're in their mid-twenties.

RULE #144
DRUNKS ERR I MEAN DRINKS

WD-40 also does a nice job of removing Kool Aid stains from carpeting. Mrs. Coach Randall was babysitting our grandson Trey and allegedly he spilled his sippy cup of Kool Aid on the white living room rug. I have a hunch it was actually Mrs. Coach Randall and she spilled a glass of wine. So, I'm going to go out on a limb and say WD-40 works on wine stains as well.

Note: Spray and blot. DO NOT rub the stain that will just make it go deeper into the carpet. Keep blotting the stain until it's no longer visible and hide the wine next time.

RULE #145
PLAN B

If your efforts from Rule #144 don't work, just spill wine all over the rest of the area rug until your light colored rug is now completely red.

MAINTENANCE

RULE #146
TOOLS

Tell your campus maintenance crew that the WD-40 website says that the product "works well on shovels, sprinkler heads, rakes, and wheelbarrows as a light lubricant, rust preventative and cleaner.

WD-40 is often used to coat tools before storing them and is also beneficial against rain and water damage because it prevents rust."

RULE #147
BOATS

A little trick I learned when I was running my charter sport fishing business (pre-coaching career) on Long Island is that WD-40 is great at getting barnacles off the bottom of boats.

Just coat the whole area with a lot of WD-40 and wait a few minutes. It loosens them up so much all you need is a putty knife to scrape the barnacles right off. If you've got a bad case of barnacles, you may need to do this a couple of times but it will make your life a lot easier.

After the last round of this procedure rub the area down with some ultra-fine sandpaper to smooth out the finish.

RULE #148
FROZEN

A former assistant coach of mine moved to Maine and it was so cold up there one October that his mailbox frozen shut. *(I think winter starts around Labor Day up there)* He sprayed some WD-40 on the hinges of it and then smacked the mailbox a couple times with a hammer. It worked like a charm.

MISCELLANEOUS

WD-40 IS ALSO GREAT AT:

RULE #149

Removing gum from the bottoms of your shoes

COACH MORGAN RANDALL

RULE #150

Sharpening and cleaning scissors

RULE #151

Opening rusty padlocks

RULE #152

Defrosting your windshield (seriously, it repels water)

RULE #153

Preventing your car doors from freezing shut. (spray it along the rubber seals around the doors)

RULE #154

Loosening stuck zippers

RULE #155

Waterproofing cleats and shoes (spray it on and don't wipe it off, let it soak in and dry)

RULE #156

Removing toilet bowl stains
(often used when rule #17 is broken)

RULE #157

Unsticking stuck piano keys

RULE #158

Removing bugs from your windshield and bumpers

RULE #159

Prevents bathroom mirrors from fogging up (spray it on a rag and wipe the mirror down with it)

RULE #160
#DIVISIONONEPROBLEMS

*Since most of us Division Three folk have to eat with our hands or plastic utensils this doesn't apply to us. But Division One coaches should know that WD-40 is great for restoring tarnished silverware. We exclusively use sporks in the Randall house so the only reason I know this tip is because the wife of a Division one coach I know shared it with me. He was too big time to speak to me but she was friendly.
(They're probably divorced.)

Just spray down your silver utensils with a little coat of WD-40 and let it sit for about 10 minutes and then wipe them off with a washcloth soaked in warm water.

**We now resume your regularly scheduled programming.
(Oh and you're welcome.)*

RULE #163
COVER YOUR @$$

Buy a book of receipts at a restaurant supply or office supply store. Keep it in your desk for those times when you lose a receipt from a trip and need to get reimbursed.

Also comes in handy at the end of the budget year in the rare event you have money left over. Take an imaginary recruiting trip, submit the mileage and expenses by filling out the blank receipts.

RULE #164
FITNESS & SAFETY TIP:

Most car accidents happen within 2 miles of home. So instead of parking in your garage, park your car 2 miles away and walk to it.

RULE #165
TOO LAZY TO IRON AND WANT FREE DRY CLEANING

Hang a wrinkled shirt or dress in the bathroom before you take a hot shower. The steam will help get the wrinkles out.

RULE #166
ROLL 'EM IF YOU GOT 'EM.

When packing, military roll your clothes.
It will save space and prevent wrinkles.

*If you don't know what military roll means, just go to YouTube and search military roll clothing. You'll never fold your clothes again after being introduced to this, especially not when traveling.

RULE #167
FITNESS TIP:

To work out your core, bear crawl on the treadmill.

RULE #168
REGARDING HATS

Baseball hats should always be worn in the direction your life is headed.

RULE #169

WHAT HAPPENS AT THE NATIONAL CONVENTION GOES ON TMZ.

Being a coaching professional is a full-time career. You don't have the luxury of clocking out when you step off the field. Everything you do can and will potentially be held against you by administrators, opposing coaches, helicopter parents and disgruntled players who sit the bench.

Your reputation is earned 24 hours a day, 7 days a week, 365 days a year. Your reputation doesn't get to take a day off. Don't do anything you wouldn't want your athletic director, university president or your wife to see on national television or the front page of the New York Times.

In other words don't get drunk and make an ass out of yourself when you go out of town on the annual pilgrimage to the national coaches convention. Same goes for casual hook ups. Just don't do it.

Always put forth the kind of demeanor that would land you in the Hall of Fame not the Hall of Shame.

RULE #170
NUTRITION TIP:

When counting calories if you have to use a calculator, you're probably eating way too much.

RULE #171
LESS THAN A BENJAMIN A WEEK.

If you can learn to live off less than a hundred bucks a week you'll be able to afford to stay in the coaching profession.

Stick with me here, the key to success when working in the coaching profession isn't about making more money, it's about needing less. Ideally the majority of your paycheck isn't spent paying down your bills. We all know you don't get rich in the coaching profession unless you coach Division One and those jobs are hard to come by. (Plus you sort of have to mortgage your soul.)

Whether you're a volunteer assistant, graduate assistant, assistant coach or head coach at any level below D-1 this rule is mission critical for your survival.

If you're on a ten month contract and don't get a paycheck in the summer, the best thing you can do is over pay your bills heading into the summer months or pay them off completely. Better yet, don't get them to begin with.

When I was a young assistant coach I worked as a bartender in the Hamptons at nights and on weekends as much as possible during the academic year so I could pay my rent and bills in advance for the entire summer. This allowed me to spend all summer traveling to camps and recruiting events without having to worry about bills piling up at home.

An even more frugal method would be to avoid having a lease or rent payment by intentionally being homeless. While I know some coaches who have done this and successfully couch surf this is not something I'd advise you do. If you're so inclined, believe it or not there's actually an app for that:
www.couchsurfing.com

RULE #172
KEEP YOUR TRAVEL PARTY TO A MINIMUM

You might want to bring additional student-managers, tutors, the equipment manager or perhaps the team's faculty advisor wants to travel with you. These people expect to be fed, housed and in some cases paid. Plus they take up space on the bus and in hotel rooms.

Your goal for road trips, besides winning games, is to keep your costs to a minimum and the cost for all the aforementioned people will come out of your budget which is too small to begin with.

The only thing worse than traveling with these extra people is when you have eight of them on your travel list but only two of them show up. That's three extra hotel rooms you just ate the cost on because it's too late to cancel.

RULE #173

JUST LIKE WITH A HEALTHY LAWN… AFTER YOU CUT YOUR HAIR, PUT THE CLIPPINGS BACK ON YOUR HEAD.

RULE #174
SIMPLE BEATS COMPLEX.

Whether it's the end of a quarter, the end of the halftime, the end of the game or an overtime possession—KEEP IT SIMPLE.

Your players already have a heightened sense of pressure given the circumstances, don't add to it. Call a simple play that involves as few people touching the ball as possible. Your team is just like a piece of machinery, the less variables in play the less factors that can cause errors.

Don't try to show off your coaching genius because you don't get style points or points on the scoreboard for "trying". The objective in a tie game or late game situation where you need a goal is flawless execution. If your players can't pull it off flawlessly in practice, don't even think about calling that play in a game. Especially with the amount of game film that's out there today, your team's botched performance will haunt you forever on YouTube.

RULE #175
NEVER LET YOURSELF GET TOO COMFORTABLE.

A coach's life is filled with ups and downs, wins and losses and you're constantly on the go. If you're enjoying a great deal of success at your current job you'll get offers to move up to the next level. And on the flipside if you're not having much success you may get canned and have to go back to coaching at a lower level or go back to being an assistant coach again.

Don't allow yourself to get too spoiled with posh facilities and unlimited resources. Just be thankful and enjoy the journey. Success comes in waves.

RULE #176
BUDGET SAVER

Buy one slice of pizza, cut it in half.
Now you have two pieces of pizza.

<u>Fun Fact:</u> If you fold your pizza slice in half, it's half the calories. This is why calzones and Stromboli are basically diet pills.

RULE #177

IF YOU WERE BORN AFTER 1980 DON'T COMPLAIN ABOUT THE COACHING PROFESSION "NOT BEING WHAT IT USED TO BE".

There has always been corruption in athletics. The day that a big time booster figured out he could make a buck and wield a ton of influence over coaches, athletic directors and university presidents is the day athletics became corrupt.

Yes, parents have gotten worse than they were a generation ago. Helicopter parents, snow plow parents, lawn mower parents or whatever you want to call them are here to stay. We all need to adapt.

The key to a successful coaching career is to recruit good players, develop them, win games and graduate them. Give the student body, faculty and fans a reason to want to buy a ticket and support your program. Build a community around your program and you will become a dynasty.

RULE #178

DON'T ASK COMPANIES TO SPONSOR YOU IF YOU'RE NOT WINNING.

Coaches all want endorsement deals. And most will solicit different apparel and sporting goods companies to sponsor them. Brands like Nike, Adidas or Under Armour all look at your team as a walking, talking advertisement for their product. If you're not winning games and no one is buying tickets to attend your games you're not a good investment to them.

When asking for sponsorship, first make sure your program is enjoying success and let the company know your team uses and loves their product. Brand loyalty counts for a lot and it engenders good will that helps grease the wheels towards them offering you a sponsorship deal. Show them the reach of your program, how many states you travel to on your schedule, the size of your social media following and the average attendance at each game.

RULE #179
FEELING DEPRESSED OR JUST IN A BAD MOOD?

Watch the Kardashians on TV and you will feel 100% better about your own life.

RULE #180
TIME SAVING

To make your breakfast even faster put the cereal directly in your morning coffee.

*Note To Millennials: If you're not that hungry and have some Tide Pods sitting around the kitchen believe it or not they can also be used as laundry detergent.

RULE #181
DATING TIP:

Guys, if you want a woman to like you make sure to buy her lots of pets. I just read that women love a man that can give them multiple organisms.

RULE #182
TURN THE VOLUME TO ZERO.

Research has shown that this is the most effective way to enjoy Justin Bieber's music.

FINAL THOUGHTS

Write down your values and go live them. Surround yourself with people who share those same values as you. There are lots of low integrity situations hidden in the coaching profession. Be aware of them, avoid them and avoid people who are involved in them.

It's better to lose than to lose your integrity. Do what's right and let the consequences follow.

OTHER BOOKS BY COACH RANDALL

If you've enjoyed reading *Randall's Rules volume one* you will also love *Randall's Rules volume two and* the many other books in the Participation Trophy Book series by Coach Morgan Randall. More information is available at:
ParticipationTrophyBooks.com

If you've enjoyed reading *Randall's Rules* you will also love the many other books in the Participation Trophy Book series by Coach Morgan Randall. More information is available at: **ParticipationTrophyBooks.com**

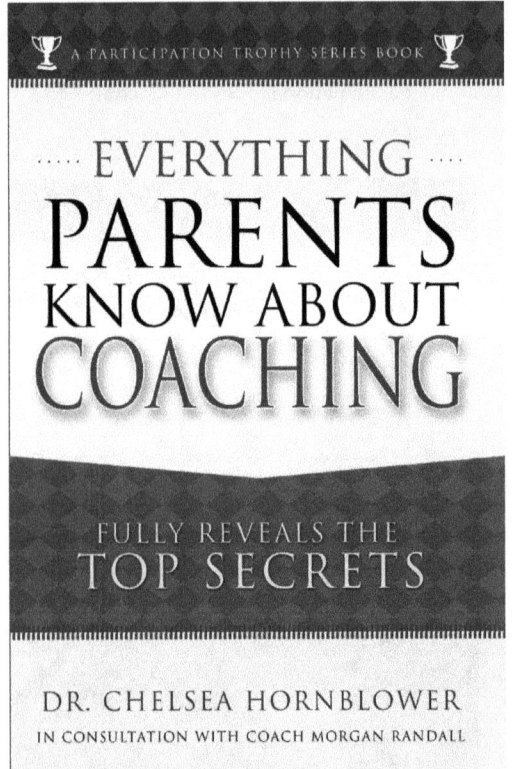

Do your players have an uncontrollable urge to sleep through practice? Do they sometimes struggle to find the motivation to attend practice?

If so, they may be suffering from a condition known as EPA or Excessive Practice Absence. These symptoms also coincide with: difficulty holding yourself accountable, not understanding your role and shirking responsibilities on your team. For help treating their case of EPA buy this book and also go to:
AccountabilityIssues.com

www.ingramcontent.com/pod-product-compliance
Lightning Source LLC
Chambersburg PA
CBHW070930160426
43193CB00011B/1643